Time Management Secrets

A Proven Step by Step Methodology
to
Getting the Things Out You Want from
Life

Copyright © 2023 Leslie Abbott

Table of Contents

Introduction

Dear friend,

You may wonder, why the heck do you need a time management product? When there is so much to be learned and so many things to get done, why should you invest 1 - 2 - 3 - 4 - 5 hours of your time studying this course?

Well, the answer is simple. In this course, I'm going to teach you not how to save time (I don't think that you can actually save time), but how to invest your time best to get the results that truly matters for your life.

What kind of results?

- Getting done the right projects.
- Investing in your personal and professional development.
- Spending more time with your loved ones.

Or in a nutshell, to actually live life and not do the same things again and again, just to realize that years and decades past by and you've not enjoyed your money or your accomplishments a single bit.

This is my purpose here.

This is my role, to show you how to manage yourself and how to invest your time, just like you would invest money, in order to generate an outstanding ROI (return on investment) in the moment and in the future.

And you know why I don't think that you can't manage time?

Because at the end of the day, everyone gets the same 24 hours. Some people achieve amazing things in those 24 hours and some don't. Some people make tens of thousands of dollars, get married, spends the most outstanding day with their kids, teaches his 4-year-old how to play baseball, writes down an important chapter for his book.

Others get caught down into unimportant trivia, focus on tasks that make no difference, play business, waste time on TV, waste time with the wrong, toxic people and are not better off at the end of the day than at the start of it.

And this is an important fact to remember - each day you get 24 hours. The purpose of these 24 hours is not to waste them on TV, on toxic people or on low quality experiences but to be better off at the end of the day than at the start of it.

To be a better person, no matter if it's financially, emotionally, mentally, physically. And to make someone's else life's better.

So, this is what I'm going to offer you, my friend. A way to manage yourself and your day in order to make an investment in your life, not an withdraw. An investment which eventually will return an outstanding reward.

What is time management?

Time management, in its most basic form, is the art of creating lists. You create a list, then you do the task on each list, then you are productive.

It is something taught virtually to everyone.

And this is effective. At least in theory. Because in practice, any kind of achievement in life, no matter the goals do not come from getting more done in a shorter period of time.

It comes from getting the right things done, at the right time, with a reasonable sense of quality. And this is where most people are wrong.

Almost every person today focuses on getting more done. Finish that project, make that call, clean the task, pick up the kids from school and so on. Almost every one of us operate the job of three people in just 24 hours.

And this is not a good idea because being busy is very different from being successful. Being successful is all about achieving results. Being busy is just about making noise.

So, what are you going to do instead?

You are going to find your priorities, focus on them and them get them done. And you are going to let everything else fall between the cracks.

Before you shout "what, are you insane, do you know what would happen if I wouldn't be here to do this every day?" I have something to say to you.

And this is that something will fall between the cracks eventually anyway. If you have only 24 hours in a day and you've got tasks that are taking you 40 hours (not considering sleep and rest), you will still have to give up at something.

You will still have to eventually delay on something, procrastinate on something and so on. So, if you are going to do it anyway, why don't you do it on the tasks that matters the less?

You know, managing your life is like fighting a war. You have missions. These missions may range from completing an entire chapter for your new book or to clean the fridge. There are more missions than you have soldiers available (in this case, soldiers meaning your time, your energy and your will-power).

So instead of focusing your soldiers on those missions that may be easier to accomplish but will eventually lose you the war, you can let them fail and focus on the things that will actually win you the war and get you back home victories.

The stuff that really matters are creating leverage in your life, cultivating relationships, taking care of your body, improving your practical and mental skills, pursuing your top goals and so on.

Yes, you'll feel bad because you've let so many things fall. Actually, you'll let about 80% of all of your tasks go uncompleted and you'll focus on the most important 20%. But guess what - you'll feel 100 times worse if you let what's truly important fall.

You know, if you hit your hand really bad, your first concern is not your shirt or to post this on Twitter. Your first concern is to stop the bleeding and get to someone who can you help you.

Because you would rather lose a shirt and some fast attention than getting your hand infected and having to go through surgery afterwards.

And here you'll learn how to take care of that hand as often as possible, without caring about the "should do" tasks.

Why do you need a time management philosophy?

The answer is simple. Your life is limited by the number of years you are going to live. You may live 75 years or you may live 100. You may even reach up to 125. But you are going to die someday.

Because your time on this Earth is limited, no matter your religious beliefs, you must make the most out of it. You must design and build the best life possible you can in the shortest amount of time and enjoy the ride.

Most people don't really understand this. Most people live as they are going to live forever and they take no interest in investing their current time for the future. They are waking up each morning, doing the same things, going to the same job, getting home doing the same thing and the cycle repeats the next day.

And they will eventually wake up that they are 40, broke, divorced and without a direction in life.

This is why you need a time management philosophy that is more than creating a list. You want to generate the best results as soon as possible and reap your rewards. You should want to know where your life is heading (goals and planning) and then discover the best tasks and targets you must hit (complete) each day in order to get closer to that point.

And yes, I know that life can be very, very unpredictable. Yes, I know, man plans, God laughs. But believe me, if disaster strikes, it will strike both if you are prepared or not. So, if that dreaded moment will come when something really bad will happen, it's far better to be prepared, financially, emotionally, physically than to feel like you have no escape.

(Just because you've bought this book, I know that you are not the type of person to lay dead and accept his faith if something bad happens.)

So, what is the time management philosophy that you'll learn?

This philosophy is based on the fact that you are human. And as a human being, you can't work as a robot. You can't just create a plan and execute it with 100% efficiency. There are things in play as motivation, will power, bio-chemistry and so on.

So here you will discover a system that is tailored to you as a person and which will focus on every area of your life (physical, emotional, mental, spiritual) and which if followed properly, will not only make you more productive, but will change your entire life in less than three months.

The "saving time" vs. "producing results" debate.

When the industrial revolution started, time management took birth. Then, it was a world where most people did things by hand disrupted by the fact that now a machine could produce a fixed number of items per hour at a higher quality.

So, in the past, if a worker produced 15 widgets per hour, then time management was used to make him produce 20 widgets per hour. And this worked great, the tasks were repetitive, the outcomes were relatively the same and with bribes, a better environment or simply by threat, workers could improve their output dramatically.

Fast forward in 2022. Now we are not producing widgets anymore. The industrial world focuses more and more on computers than on human input. And with small exceptions, no one really cares how many widgets you produce per hour (unless you are working at a burger stand).

No, in 2022, it's all about being a knowledge worker. You work in front of a computer and you need to find ways to solve different problems. You need to improve the shipping times of a cargo or you need to motivate a certain department for better results. You need to manage a group of people who you need to fix an IT problem.

You don't need to fix two IT problems in an hour and if you want a promotion, upgrade to three. You don't need to do repetitive tasks again and again and be paid based on the number of how many of them you actually do.

Instead, as I've said, it's all about fixing problems and finding solutions to challenges. Solutions to be faster, of better quality, more profitable. Solutions to cost less when produced or to improve brand awareness.

And your sole job is to find these solutions as good as possible, not find as many solutions as you can. You don't need to create

100 wheels as in the past, you just need to create a really awesome one and then use it.

This is why I consider the "laser targeted focus" philosophy better than "trying to save more hours into the day".

And for the person who can get the most important 20% done, that person can let everything else slip, can come late at work, can sometimes make error, can spend more time with his family, can spend more times with his hobbies. He's the result maker while everyone else is pretending to work.

Time is neutral

Time can neither be saved or won, it's just an illusion.

Let me give you an example. Let's say that each day you spend 30 minutes going from point A to point B. This seems as lost time. Then you decide to buy a car and you take only 10 minutes from point A to point B.

You've saved 20 minutes. However, if you are not going to invest these 20 minutes into something useful, you could have saved the money on the car and just commute using public transport.

The idea here is simple - you can save time by doing things faster but if you don't invest it into something useful, it's still lost time. Yes, you can finish by 4 PM and you have one hour to waste, but if you use that hour on Facebook instead on something useful, it's still lost time.

So, what should you do instead?

Try to invest every moment into something useful. For example, in the above scenario, you can spend that 30 minutes to read daily. This will be time very well spent. You can use the remaining hour to work out. Etc.

The idea here is that time is saved only if it's put to good purpose.

As a good exercise, let's think for a second, how much is your time worth? For all intensive purposes we will use a monetary value here.

Is it worth $5/hour?

$15/hour?

$100/hour?

You know best, but in average, based on the average skills and payments it's about $20/hour. Now, every time you want to do something that is not an investment into your life, ask yourself "would I pay $20 to do this?".

If the answer is yes, then do it. If not, focus on something you can do that is worth at least $20/hour (this is not only a monetary value. For example, reading a book that can bring you an extra $10,000/year is an investment. Working out and feeling better each day is an investment. Spending time with your family is an investment. Just use some kind of mark to know to not waste your time).

In time, your hourly value will double, triple, increase by ten. You will ask the question "is this worth at least $100/hour?" before doing anything. Some people ask if it is worth $500/hour and so on.

But no matter what you do, no matter what is worth to you $15, $50, $100, $500/hour always remember these three things:

a) Invest in yourself.

b) Invest in your family and loved ones.

c) Invest in your future.

This is the quickest and easiest way to achieve groundbreaking success.

The things you are going to find in this course.

There are five modules in this course. Each one of them will cover one specific area of time and life management. Then there are three bonuses that can be easily consumed.

In total, you should be able to finish everything in under 4 - 5 hours. However, here's an important thing.

Each module comes with practical action steps to take. Please, please, do not move forward with the next module until you have actually gone through the exercises.

Just knowing these things on an intellectual level it's good, but your life will never change if you don't actually apply them.

Conclusion

I hope you've enjoyed this quick introduction into the course. Now, starting tomorrow, please go through one module each two or three days. Some modules will require a lot more time as the exercises you are going to do tend to get more intense after a while.

But remember, your goal here is not to finish this as soon as possible. Your goal is to change your life.

Module 1 – Personal Management Vs. Time Management

A Proven Step by Step Methodology

to

Getting the Things Out You Want from Life

by Leslie Abbott

Introduction

Welcome to the first module

In this module, we are going to cover how habits (the things you do again and again) are the most important force shaping your life. Your habits brought where you are now and only by changing your habits you can become a new person.

Money, love, success is something you attract by the person you become. I'm not talking about the law of attraction here. I'm talking about common sense - a confident person attracts other confident people. A smart person attracts smart people. An ambitious person attracts other ambitious people.

But how do you become the kind of person that attracts only good things in his life? Well, as I've said before, by creating the rituals and habits that will eventually transform you into that person. You can't become a person of value overnight. You need to go through a process, and by having the right habits, that process will be much shorter.

So, sit tight and be prepared to change the fabric of your life - for the better.

You are not really in control of your life!

My good friend, what I may say in the following line may offend you. Please do not take any offense. I've seen this happening both on myself, my loved one and everyone around us.

And to be more specific, I've seen how we are being lived, how we are being driven like sheep in a direction or another on a day-to-day basis than actually using our brain and making each day unique and fulfilling.

Let's take an example. What do you do first thing in the morning? Well, I've seen many people who've first thing is to check email, before even washing their teeth. Why? Because it's a habit.

It's not a habit that serves them but it's a habit. Let's take something else - the average American family spends around 4 hours a day watching TV. That's 28 hours a week. 28 hours each week, a little over a complete day just watching TV.

Why? Because it's a habit.

More and more people are smoking when they are drinking their coffee. They don't even need to smoke. I understand the need to smoke in a tensioned situation but they are smoking just for the sake of it.

More and more people spend more time on Facebook than on their work.

More and more people multi-task instead of focusing on a single high importance task.

Why? As I've said, they are all negative habits. Now, how these habits were formed, it doesn't really matter. What matters is that if you want to be a champion, if you want to get the most out of your life, you need to replace them with positive habits.

What are positive habits?

Well ... let's take a look:

- Working out each morning.

- Drinking at least two liters of water each day.

- Reading for a few minutes before sleep instead of watching TV.

- Spending less than 15 minutes a day on social media.

- Walking for short distances instead of taking a cab.

- Waking up early and refreshed.

- Eating at least occasionally very healthy food.

- Smiling to other people.

- Etc.

There are virtually hundreds of positive habits you can have. But what does this have to do with a time management book?

Well, these are the things that you do again and again, on a daily basis. And if you replace the negative habits with positive ones, you will get better results on a day-to-day basis.

But you may think that you can control yourself and that negative habits are not a problem. You know, I've used to think the same thing. Until I've realized that habits are like driving.

After a while you don't realize that you've done them until you've done them. You don't realize in the moment when you open the TV or check Facebook. You realize only after you've lost three hours doing this.

The first step to change your life and become more productive (productive as in producing more) is to identify and change your habits. Once you do this, the rest becomes very, very easy.

Habit is destiny (in a good or bad way).

Let's take a simple example.

John and Andrew are two usual folks. They earn about the same sum of money and they live very similar life.

John decides to change something. He is satisfied with his life but he wants a little more. On the other hand, Andrew just keeps doing what he's been always doing.

So, John decides to only add 15 minutes of exercise each day. In the first day John enjoys the exercise but sees no payoff. However, after a week, he is feeling better than ever. Because he is feeling better, he decides to eat healthier. This leads in turn to a better mental focus.

With his new found clarity, he starts reading specialty and self-development book. He becomes an expert at his job (sales). This brings him a promotion. Soon after, he quits and starts his own sales company. His entire life changes.

I know, it may sound very far-fetched but please suspend your disbelief for a moment. I've seen similar scenarios happen. A single good habit, done daily, can produce amazing improvements in the future. Reading daily or working out or simply journaling daily can improve you so much that you won't recognize yourself anymore.

On the other hand, let's take a negative habit - drinking each evening just a little glass. That glass will lead in turn to two glasses and so on. Soon you would find yourself at rehab, trying to get rid of a drinking addiction even if you don't even understand when this happened.

Now, it's very hard to understand what habits you have on a day-to-day basis. For example, when I was trying to discover this, I got into a state of denial that I'm not actually doing this. only when I have been filmed, I've finally accepted what is happening.

(And even there, even if on a logical level I was true to myself, on a emotional one, I was still in denial).

Exercise: what kind of habits are governing your life?

This is a very quick exercise, but you need to follow my steps exactly.

1. Please go to someone who knows you really well and ask him or her to tell you the truth about your habits, ask to be more exact what kind of negative patterns of behavior are you showing?

2. Install a time tracking application on your computer and review your computer using habits after one week. You would be surprised to see where all your time goes.

3. Ask yourself - what kind of person do you want to become and write that down. Now that you know this critical piece of info, think of three habits or rituals you can do daily to get closer to that person.

(A quick note here - one habit takes about 31 days to become natural. After 31 days you will do it automatically, like driving. However, because the brain does not accept change so easily, it's best to keep building only one habit at a time.

So, for example, if you want to get into the habit of reading daily, then do this for 31 days without trying to build another habit. Once this habit is built, you can move to the next one. I've almost always failed when I've tried to build more than one habit).

To change your life, start now.

Most people tend to wait a lot of time until they decide to change their habits. However, changing your habits is like trying to lose weight. You can't do it in one day or one week. It will take some time; a lot more than you would want.

But you are doing it for that moment in the future, no matter if it's after one month or six when you've finally given up on that bad habit. So, if you truly want to improve, if you truly want to get control of your life, start right now.

I haven't covered one important point here - how to get rid of a negative habit. Well, even if the methods are controversial, I suggest you use leverage. What is leverage? Anything that works in your favor. Let me explain.

Let's say that you want to quit smoking. This is usually something very hard to do. You could say to yourself that smoking kills, that smoking costs a lot of money and so on. This rarely works as this information is printed on every pack of cigars.

However, you can also use leverage. To be more exact, carry a small bottle with you. Each time you smoke, put the remaining's there. After one week, take a look at how much trash gathered there.

You would be amazed. And if you want to make the effect even stronger, to add a very negative emotion to smoking, try to smell that. You will probably get sick and throw up, but you will not smoke anytime soon.

It's not pleasant, but it works and, in the end, this is all that matters.

Keep your mind clear.

Another important thing required to get awareness and manage yourself is to keep your mind clear. You see, your mind is not a very good computer. It can store virtually an infinite amount of information but it comes with a very small RAM memory. This means that the more you try to remember, the harder it will be to store anything new.

This is why I suggest that each day, at the end of the day, journal. You may throw away the paper or delete the document, you are not doing it for recording purposes (even if it's worth it). You are doing it to clear your mental screen from all the information that piled up during the day - information that are keeping the space occupied for what's truly important.

And as a matter of fact, if you want to be more creative and more productive, record everything and keep your mind as clear as possible.

You can use tools as Evernote (www.evernote.com) to record websites, screen captures, notes and a lot more, you can use a voice recorder to "download" every important thought you may have in your head for later processing, you may use a notebook to jot down what's important to you and so on.

Just don't keep it in your head. Even entire productivity systems like GTD by David Allens are based on this concept. I don't know if you need to take it so far as GTD (it's an efficient system though), but I suggest that you empty your mind at least twice a day.

Exercise: Clearing your mind

The following exercise is very, very simple. Please pick up a blank piece of paper (or open a new document) and write down virtually everything that is on your mind. Everything, from the overdue bill to the holiday you look forward to go. Then pick the ten most important things from that list and try to focus on getting them done so you can have peace of mind.

Tracking means improving

As I've said earlier, we don't know that we've did a thing until we've actually done it.

For example, very many people have a problem with impulsive buying. Even if they are in debt, if they see something they like, they will buy it and regret it at home. Their mind becomes "locked down" during that phase and even if they know that it's not a good idea to buy it, they will still do.

So here's what I suggest. Keep a track of the habit you are trying to kill. If you want to save money, if you want to be more disciplined and responsible with your money, the key is simple.

Get a small notebook and write down every time you spend money. It doesn't matter if you buy a cup of coffee or a new stereo. Write down virtually every purchase you make. Two things will happen.

The first one, you'll become so tired of writing it down that you will stop buying just to go through the process once again.

The second is that once you can see for yourself how much you spend, you will have a real alarm and real proof of your behavior, acting as leverage to help you stop.

This can apply to virtually anything, not just spending money - unhealthy eating, TV, Facebook, computer games and so on.

Exercise: Track one negative habit

I would like you to go buy a notebook and find the habit that is most damaging to your life. This may be anything from smoking to arguing too much.

Make a commitment to write down every time you do this and actually do it. And if someone asks what you are doing, simply say that you want to jot down something important before you forget it.

Conclusion

My dear friend, we are at the end of this module. In this module I've tried to show you that you are not really in control of your life and that if you truly want to control your life, you need to control the building blocks, which are habits.

I hope you have completed the exercises and if you haven't, please go back and so.

Module 2 – Anti-Procrastination Secrets

A Proven Step by Step Methodology
to
Getting the Things Out You Want from Life

by Leslie Abbott

Introduction

If I were to guess what is the biggest fault or mistake people are making to bring misery in their own life this is procrastination. Procrastination is knowing what to do and not doing it.

When you procrastinate, it doesn't really matter what tools are you using or what time management system you are employing. You can organize your tasks in the most efficient manner possible, but if you are not acting on them, it's all for nothing.

You can have the perfect project plan. You can have in front of you a plan that will make you a millionaire. You can have the perfect recipe for an amazing life. But if you don't put in your time and energy in it, then it's all for nothing.

So, in this chapter, we are going to try to find some solutions for your procrastination. Solutions that may not always work, but if combined, will usually give you that burst of energy and motivation to get started.

And as a matter of fact, if you simply get started on a task, the hardest part is done. I can't remember how many times I've dreaded to get started on a task just to finish it in 15 minutes without any of the pain I've imagined.

Actually, you know, the easiest way to beat procrastination is just to set the timer to 30 minutes (also known as the

Pomodoro technique - found at Pomodorotechnique.com) and make a promise to yourself to work for 30 minutes no matter what. That's all. 30 minutes. The project may take 5 hours, but commit just for 30 minutes.

And sometimes you'll work only 30 minutes. But most of the time, that initial boost will lead to another 30 minutes session. And another. And another. And soon you find yourself working full time on your most important task.

So even if procrastination is something that starts inside of you and not an external problem, I hope that these tips can help you overcome it.

Why we procrastinate?

This is a very complex question with no easy answer.

But if I were to give the simplest answer is because the pain of doing something is bigger than the pain of not doing it. This pain can be real or not real. Can be physical or emotional or spiritual or mental. Can be the pain that something more important is on the top of your mind.

And where I mean important here, I don't mean important in a general sense. For example, it may be important for you to see a certain movie or to waste time in a certain way. Important is usually what gives you pleasure or relief.

For example, if you are a gamer and you need to take care of project X but in the same time you want to finish some level in a game, then you'll do the one which gives you the greatest pleasure - procrastinating on project X.

So now comes the question - "so if I don't enjoy my work, I'll never get it done"?

Not really. We work for a reward. This is usually money or recognition. However, when that reward is not enticing enough, then we can use the carrot and the stick system to motivate ourselves, a system I'm going to show you in just a few seconds.

Pain vs. Pleasure

Do you know the carrot and the stick system? If you want to make a donkey move, you can simply either slap him with a stick or hang a carrot in front of him. The first method works sometimes, the second works most of the time.

Here's how you can apply this to your own life - create consequences for achieving or not achieving a certain task. How do you do this particularly?

It's simple. Ask a friend to keep you accountable. You will say something like this to him:

"Here's what I've got to do. Here's $100. In 3 days (or whatever is the deadline), I must get this done or you can keep the money and spend it on whatever you like. Under no circumstances can you return me the money if I don't complete the task".

If you want to make this even more appealing, use $250, $500, $1000 whatever works for you. The idea is simple, you either do it or you'll suffer very grave consequence. Now, I know that this is not in your comfort zone. Actually, it took me some time to actually apply it.

But once you do, you'll notice something amazing happening. Your procrastination will disappear. You will say to yourself "I must get this done, no matter what, or I'll lose the money".

Now, you must also get it done the right way, so in your wager, you can add some quality requirements too. You don't want just to rush and get it done; you want to get it done right.

This can be used in several ways. The idea is to add something painful that you must do as you are forced to do it (don't rely on your honor system, just force yourself this way) if you don't complete the task.

On the other hand, you can also add some kind of reward - if I do this, I'll not only get my $100 back, but I can also do something I want. Now, this is a little tricky as you may fall into the mindset "but I can do this whenever I want", so it's also good here to use some leverage.

What kind of leverage? Make a deal with a friend or whatever that if you do x, you'll get y in return. It may be the fact that he borrows you his car or that he'll take you Paintball (on your money, of course). Just use whatever kind of leverage you can to force yourself to get the job done.

Will power and motivation alone works, but before you can get there, you need to push through the resistance.

Your inner beliefs

As I've said earlier, we are not really in control of our life. Next to habits, there is one more thing that is influencing our life - actually, the thing that is actually influencing our habits.

And these are our beliefs. Our beliefs are what we believe of things. It's what we think that is right or wrong, what brings us pleasure and what brings us pain. And based on these beliefs, we manage everything we do each day.

Example - do you have a strong belief that you need to sleep 10 hours a day to be rested? Then you'll do so. Do you have the belief that each day must be an investment for the future and you must not waste a single moment? You'll do that too.

Beliefs determine virtually everything we do on a basic level. If our life is a table, then your beliefs are the legs that is holding that table.

If you build the right beliefs, then your life will be extraordinary. But what do you do when you build the wrong beliefs - like people are bad, the world is a cold place, I'm ugly, I'm always sick, etc.

Well, there are two steps to that. First you try to discover why you think this. This is usually related to some kind of experience that made you think this way. It may be something recent or something ten years ago.

Second, you create a scenario that will prove it otherwise and then you go out and do it, proving and programming your subconscious mind that your belief is wrong. For example, if you think that no one appreciates you, then you find ways to be appreciated and you take great delight in this as often as possible.

Does it always work?

No. But it works most of the time. I've also tried NLP (Nero-linguistic programming) to change beliefs and while it may be an efficient method, it did not work as planned for me. I find the simple action of proving yourself otherwise, of building success on success to be a lot more effective.

Exercise: Determine your limiting beliefs

I would like you to take a new blank piece of paper / document and then write down how you see the world and yourself. Then I would like to pull up the old exercise where you've wrote how your ideal life would look like.

Now, please identify the kind of beliefs that you must give up in order for the first image to be a little more similar to the second. Focus on the top three.

Write down why you think this way. Write down in detail, I've wrote up to 40 pages on one belief alone. And finally, create a plan to not feel this way anymore, to prove to your brain the opposite.

Get to work. Good luck! Don't be in a hurry!

Finding Your Why

Usually, when you don't want to do something, it's because you don't have a strong enough why behind you. Let me give you an example (which was overused by now, so you may know it).

Let's say that I set a plank between two chairs, a foot above the ground and I ask you to walk for 3 feet until the end. At the end, you will get $100.

Will you, do it? Most people would, it's easy money.

Now let's say that I do the same thing but I raise the plank 5 feet into the air. Would you still do it? Chances are that you would.

Again, easy money. You know what you want, your why is very simple and the pain is relatively low.

But let's say that I raise the same plank between two skyscrapers and I promise you $1.000.000 if you would walk. Would you, do it?

Hell no. You would call me insane.

Your reason why for doing this is not strong enough for taking the risk and the pain. But what if your kids were kidnapped and you would have to walk to the other side to rescue them or lose them forever?

You would do it in an instant, without even second thoughts.

This is the power of your "why". When you can't find yourself to do something, ask yourself, why do you want to do that and don't stop until you find an answer good enough to push you until the end.

When the why gets clearer, the how gets easier - don't ever forget that.

You don't need to get pumped up

Temporary motivation is one of the most dangerous things I ever saw. If you listen to a good song, a motivational speech and you want to take over the world, then you are not the only one.

But you see what's the real problem here?

It's the fact that your motivation will fade away really fast, way before you can achieve anything worthwhile. So, while I encourage motivational speeches, I consider that motivation that starts from inside of you is a far better way to go.

And how do you find that inner motivation?

Here's the best exercise ever - similar to the one above.

Get a piece of paper (or several sheets) and write down your life purpose. Write a minimum of 500 answers. This may take you one hour, one day or one week. It may take you even one month. But write 500 answers.

But the 500th answer, you will know why you are doing what you are doing and you will be motivated do to it until the very end.

Procrastination damage control list.

Below I will show you a few tools that you can use each time you find yourself procrastinating. These tools are very simple to use but you must actually use them.

Here is the list:

- Just go to work for 15 minutes then stop. This is usually enough to give you a boost.

- Go take a walk and clear your mind.

- Exercise - exercising gives you clarity.

- Write down on a piece of paper why you want to do this task. Don't stop until you find a strong enough reason why.

- Write down on a piece of paper everything that is concerning you - so you can have a clear head.

- Ask a friend to keep you accountable using the system I've shown you above.

- Change the location, try to work from somewhere else.

- If you work from a computer, try to work on paper or get away from the PC.

- Cut down the Internet connection.

There are far more methods, but if you use just a few of these ones when you procrastinate, then you will eventually get over the obstacle. Remember, pain is temporary, glory is forever. If you must do it, do it, no matter if you want or not.

This is a quote that I came up with on my own many years ago. Yes, it's Copyrighted.

Procrastination is the Ruination of a Nation

Later I added 'Get er done'!

The point is this. If you fail to plan or act – you can only blame yourself when things fall apart.

I wonder how many nations were destroyed over the centuries because they thought they still had time before the invading armies took them by surprise in the darkness of the night.

Best to just get it done quickly and efficiently.

Conclusion

Now, the best way to put this module to use is to actually go and work on a task you've delayed for a long time. Find that task, use the tools found here and get to work. Go, go, go!

Module 3 – Life Management 101

A Proven Step by Step Methodology

to

Getting the Things Out You Want from Life

by Leslie Abbott

Introduction

Life is a blessing. Even with all the problems that appear each day, it is still a blessing. It's an adventure where you can't truly control anything but you should feel fortunate for living.

In this chapter, I am going to try to teach you how you can get the most out of it. I'm going to show you how to create goals while keeping the habit to live in the moment. Because if you always live for something far away in the future, you will always be stressed and upset.

The idea is to live right now, right here. The idea is that you are not creating goals for what these goals means but for the way there. For the fun, for the satisfaction, for the pleasure of moving towards something you want. What you actually get from your goal is only an afterthought.

You set goals for the person you become and for the journey there, not for the goals themselves.

So, I hope you will enjoy this chapter. It was my biggest pleasure writing it.

Having a balanced life

Your first goal as a human being is to be happy, not to pursuit goals. You are trying to earn money in order to be happy. You are working out to be satisfied with yourself so you can be happy.

It's that simple. Everything we do is in order to become happy. But here's something to think about - would you rather have a life that provides you with satisfaction in all areas or would you prefer to excel in one and feel miserable in others?

You know, millionaires tend to be depressed sometimes. Why? Because money themselves can buy only a certain number of things. I'm not saying that money is the root of all evil. Money is the product of the mind and it's a tool for our survival and thriving. Neither love of money is the root of all evil.

The root of all evil is fear. The root of all evil is living a life where you are always missing something and trying to fill that gap with money or sex or anything else. It may work to some degree, but it will never make you fulfilled.

So, here's what I'm suggesting instead. Try to live a balanced life. A life where you may earn $50.000 or $100.000 but you also enjoy amazing relationships, amazing health, amazing lifestyle, amazing fun.

A life that is worth living, a live lived for the sake of what's now, of what makes you happy, no matter if it's a smile from a small child or a holiday with your loved ones. Because these come way before money.

Yes, you need money, to help you survive. But you need everything else to make your life a life worth living.

So here are the areas in which you should keep a balance:

- Financial

- Career

- Health / body.

- Relationships.

- Family.

- Education.

- Lifestyle / fun.

- Traveling.

- Spiritual.

- Emotional.

And take my word for it, it's better to rank a 5 in each one of these than to rank 10 in the financial area and feel like you've sold your soul. Try to keep a balance between them and you will be happy. You will live your true-life purpose - to be happy.

Seeing the big picture

Most people tend to get bogged down into small details. The shower broke. The phone bill must be paid. They live in a constant reaction to all of this, instead of seeing their life as a whole.

As a human being, it's far easier to focus on the bad things than on the positive ones. After all, this is how evolution rigged us to survive, to notice threats and eliminate them.

But you see, small problems will always appear, no matter if you live in uptown Manhattan or in Kansas. So, you may just as well discard them and focus on the truly important things.

What are the truly important things?

Your health, your relationships, your evolution as a person. These should take first center in your life. And in order to do this, I've got a really nice exercise for you to try.

Each Sunday, make a small review of your life. Write it just as it is. You will be the only one who will read this. Write everything that's good and what's bad. And then, try to be grateful for all the good things that already exists and focus on making them even bigger, instead of wasting your valuable life on solving the smallest of problems.

This may sound as utopic but it really isn't. It's just a way to see life as it is. It's just a way to build blessings on blessings, victories on victories, instead of thinking that your life is a total disaster because you ran out of battery on your phone or if you are caught up in traffic.

It may take some time to fully realize this, but start now. See your life as it is, not as your problems. You are not your problems just as you are not your victories. You are you. A human being who deserves to be very, very happy.

How to set emotionally charged goals

Goal setting is a very controversial topic. As I've said earlier, some people hate goals. They consider that if you set goals, your focus is always on the future.

Well, I say something else. Set goals for the person you will become by achieving those goals, for the satisfaction of the journey, for the emotions you'll encounter when you'll push yourself and not for the reward.

You are not for the gold, you are for the way that will get you there to the goal (and this paradoxically will also bring you the gold, as you can give your best in the moment).

So how do you set goals?

I like to set SMART goals. Smart goals are the standard and they are usually kind of effective. And SMART stands for ...

Specific - make your goal as specific as possible so you'll know without a doubt where you are going.

Measurable - you need to know if you've got there, so it's best to quantify your goal. For example, you can't quantify in terms of numbers an ideal relationship, but you can write down how you would feel when you've found it.

Achievable - this goal must not be impossible to achieve. Based on who you are right now, this goal may be far-fetched but not truly impossible.

Realistic - this goal must be anchored into reality. Having six pack abs is possible. Having it in four weeks it's not.

Timely - a goal is just a dream with a deadline. So set a deadline to know how much time you have to get there and to give your best in this amount of time. I'm not saying that you should not give your best in everything you do, but setting a deadline virtually forces you to get started on the goal.

Here is a goal using the SMART formula:

By 15 June 2023, I will have lost 25 pounds by working out three times a week.

As I've said, the fact that you've lost 25 pounds as a consequence of this goal is important, but the fact that you've became a person that works out three times a week is far, far more important.

I'm saying this because in the end, success is something you attract by the person you become, not by the goals you set and achieve.

Exercise: Set your top five goals

Now I would like for you to take the time and write down the top five things you want in your life. As I've said, and I'll repeat myself, the goal itself is not as important as the person you'll become moment by moment to get there.

So please write down your goals and make them SMART using the formula above. Go, go, go!

Creating your vision board

Your vision board is something to remind you of the good things that are awaiting you in the future. People create vision boards using whiteboards or cork tables or screensavers or wallpapers.

How do you want to create your vision board it's your job. But here's what it should include. First of all, pick ten pictures of all the good things that already exists in your life. As I've said before, you should build success on success, happiness on happiness and not only on scarcity.

Sadness and feeling like nothing are working in your life may provide you with a motivation boost but that's all. On the other hand, wanting more of what's good is a very strong motivator.

Find these pictures and post them on your board (an exercise is coming up soon). Then pick up ten photos that should represent all areas of your life (I've told you about them one minute ago) and post them too.

And then post that board into a location where you'll see it every day. Your mind will get focused on what you want and you'll find opportunities to get there far easier than having a goal document somewhere on your computer.

Exercise: Create your e-vision board

My friend, I would like you to take the above exercise and create a vision board on your computer using Picasa from Google. Picasa offers you the option to create outstanding collages and you can use this to assemble a wallpaper or even a screensaver of what you want out of your future.

Or if you are really interested in this, you can create a vision board for each area of your life and then use it as a screensaver. Have fun, it's a very insightful exercise!

Dream to achieve

Everything good that is right now in your life was only a dream sometime. The job you may have, was only a wish or a dream sometime. The way you think right now, it was only a dream sometime in the future. The friends, the loved ones, were only a wish, a hope sometime.

And everything good that will eventually appear in your life when you don't expect it is the same. Just a dream, just a wish, that you never thought that can transform into reality but it did.

So, here's a good advice my friend, don't be afraid to dream. Don't be afraid to wish. Don't go on the idea that if you have no expectations, you won't be disappointed. Have expectations and you'll find a way to make them real. I promise.

Be yourself

You know what's the biggest mistake you can do with your life? Trying to live like someone else. You see someone, with the cars, the money and you want to be like him or her. But it would be a huge mistake to do that.

Why?

Because you are best at being yourself. Now, I'm not saying that you should not improve yourself as much as possible, but just be yourself. You are a child of God and you should remain true to yourself no matter what.

So set your own goals. Have your own dreams. Set your own way through life. It's the best way.

Conclusion

We've reached the end of this module too my friend. I don't know if you realize, but you are halfway through. Good job!

Module 4 – How to Avoid Burnout

A Proven Step by Step Methodology to Getting the Things Out You Want from Life

by Leslie Abbott

Introduction

You know what makes me laugh most? When I see someone working 20 hours a day in order to be a hero. He stays over the program, he takes work at home, he shows of to everyone how good he is.

But in reality, his results are awful. How come?

Because work does not equal results. Results are composed of your effort and how effective that effort is. So, if you work ten hours at an effectiveness level of 2, you'll get a "score" of 20.

On the other hand, if you work five hours at an effectiveness score of five, you'll get a score of 25. Half the amount of time invested, a little over the previous results.

Workaholism does not usually produce results. Yes, hard work brings a lot of good things in life. But hard work must also be effective work. And if you consider that working just to realize that you've got it all wrong the following morning is effective, then you will never become productive.

This is what we are going to cover in this chapter. We are going to cover how you can keep your mind and body in top state so you can achieve more from your workout without experiencing burnout.

Why burnout appears?

Burnout by definition is when you have worked too much and you are not effective anymore. To better understand it, it's like when you have worked an entire day and at the end of the day you are accident prone.

Usually, burnout takes place on a mental level, not a physical one. In other words, your brain can't coordinate any more efficiently.

The reasons why burnout appears are many but they are usually centered around a single one - too much work and too little rest. Now, let' me define rest.

Rest here does not mean sleeping, even if that is important. Rest means going on a idle state on your physical, emotional and mental state. This is something that most people don't do.

Why?

Because as soon as they finish work, they go to Facebook. Then they watch TV. And so on. I don't know if you realize but doing something productive and doing something unproductive requires about the same level of mental energy - you have to think in both.

And when you achieve burnout, more work won't solve it. When you've overworked yourself the only way to recover fast is to stop everything you are doing. This may sound as impossible sometimes, but if you are in a burnout state, you are going to make a lot of mistakes and you'll have to redo the work all over again.

But there is also a better solution - prevent burnout from appearing. In order to do that, you will need to create renewal rituals in the four main dimensions of your life: physical, emotional, spiritual, mental.

Your physical dimension

Your physical dimension - your body is virtually the most important out of all. Without a healthy body you cannot plant the required seeds into the future nor actually reap the rewards.

Which is a little ironic. Most people will virtually ruin their health in one way or another and then spend years of their life and all their money paying the price.

When it comes to renewing your physical dimension, there are two key components. The first one is staying fit. The second one is eating right.

Staying fit is more about being physically attractive. That comes as an afterthought actually. Staying fit is about allowing all your organs to work at full capacity so you can get the job done, whatever that job may be.

What is the standard of staying fit? You don't need to have a six-pack abs. Actually, you don't even need a good physique. You just need to work out in order to help your body work properly.

How much workout is necessary?

There is almost never anything like too much workout, but I suggest that you sweat at least 15 minutes a day. If you do this in the morning, your heart rate will go up and you will experience a boost of energy.

And if working out is not for you, then you can always try something like Yoga. Yoga is a great way to relieve stress, to clear your mind and to become more flexible.

Now let's talk about the eating right part. I'm not a big advocate of crash diets so I won't force you to live on green stuff for the rest of your life. But as a few general advices drink a lot of water (minimum two liters a day) and between that hamburger and stake, try to eat at least one salad.

If you can eat at least 1/3 green, and in green I mean alkaline food, then you will be healthy. As far as junk food and so on, it's rather hard on our body to process it, but you can eat it if you want. Just make sure you keep a balance so your body won't spend more energy processing the food than the food is actually releasing.

And if you always feel tired, one of the causes may be just this. Your body is putting so much energy into breaking down the food into valuable energy that you are not getting so much back. In that case, drink a lot of water, start eating alkaline for a while and stop drinking coffee or energy drinks to boost you up.

It may work temporarily but it will cause metabolic changes to your body in the long term.

Your emotional dimension.

Admit it or not, you live in order to feel. You live to feel pride, love, sadness, loss, etc. Feelings are the driving force of your life. Feeling of love for a person can help you change and feeling of dread or loss can help you get over an addiction.

Emotions are the most addictive chemicals in the nature. So if you want to become more productive and more motivated about something, add some feeling to it. How?

By participating into activities that will get you out of your normal emotional comfort zone. For example, if you have kids, spend one complete day with them.

If you don't have kids but you have a spouse, then try to have a night out from time to time. You would be amazed on how much energy just a night out can bring you compared to the time invested.

Each time you invest into your emotions, one hour wasted means ten productive hours, so don't be afraid and go feel alive!

Your mental dimension

I've already advocated how important is to read books and keep yourself trained in your industry. But when it comes to renewal, things are a little different.

Mental renewal is needed when your mind feels overwhelmed and you can't think clear. When you are in this situation you have a few good options.

The first one is to talk to someone or simply write down everything that concerns you. By clearing your mind, you can give your best without being sabotaged by millions of thoughts racing around every second.

The second one is to read a good piece of literature. Fiction literature is very relaxing and can calm your mind. I would also suggest self-development literature, but that will make you think and in a mental renewal phase, you need to clear, not add more.

The third one is to simply use your mind for something else than usual. If you are a manager, then take a weekend off and help someone build a house. The physical effort will flush your negative emotions, the fact that you are building the house will boost your good emotions and the "how-to" for building the house will boost your mental renewal.

Oh, and if you are not in the mood of any of these, just go to YouTube and watch an interesting documentary - something unique that is not related to your interests, hobbies or work.

Your spiritual renewal

When I'm talking about spiritual renewal here, I'm not talking about religion. You can believe in religion or not. I don't condemn anyone.

Instead, I'm talking about getting to know yourself. And how do you do that?

The best and the easiest way to do it is to meditate. Now, meditation is not easy. It requires a lot patience and I've tried it for months before it finally clicked for me. But at the end of a meditation session, you'll feel like the entire world was lifted off your shoulders. It's something hard to explain unless you actually experience it.

How do you meditate? You usually focus your attention on your breath. But because "vanilla" meditation is usually very difficult, I suggest you go to a place special to you, outside or inside, buy some guided meditation audiobooks (they are rather cheap) and just follow the instructions there.

20 minutes of meditation usually means more than 8 hours of sleep. But in order to actually understand this, you have to try it. It's one of those intangible things that you can only experience, not describe.

Creating renewal rituals

I gave you some good ideas above on how to renew your four dimensions. These are not the only ideas. You can play Tennis, you can travel, you can go volunteer, you can write in a journal and so on.

But it's important to have some renewal rituals in place. And the best way to do this is with the help of 'joes goals'. Simply enter into your browser search and see what appeals.

On this website, as I've explained in a different module, you can create habits and then assign a certain day of the week (or more) to do them.

Exercise: create your renewal rituals

Now it's time to create your own rituals. Don't worry if they are not perfect. Do whatever works for you. So please create one ritual for each dimension and start applying them as soon as possible. Remember, your well-being depends on this.

Workaholism.

Workaholism is a disease that is spreading to more and more people around the country. The main symptom is working too much and getting too little done. Avoid it like the fire.

The problem with being a workaholic is not that you are ruining your health (and life) for the company. The problem is that you are not effective enough and that if you would give 100% of your energy until 17:00, more would get done.

As a matter of fact, please try this experiment. Tomorrow, work only until 17:00 and spend the rest of the time to do whatever you want, as long as it's not related to any kind of work.

Do this for three days. Then tell me what results you've got. Chances are that your productivity doubled at least.

Sprint, not marathon.

Life and success in life is about sprinting. It's about finding those few opportunities where you'll give more than anyone else and then enjoying the results. It's not an endurance race, it's a race of speed.

So, think about this. Think about how you treat yourself on a day-to-day basis. Try to stop it. Stop it and give your best for one hour, two, three, four each day and then rest. But in those four hours, act like there is no tomorrow and do the most painful tasks you have.

And if you do this, you will soon realize that one hour of quality work is better than ten hours of appearing working.

Conclusion

We've reached the end of the module. The lesson here my good friend? To work less and more effectively and to renew your four-energy dimension as soon as possible. This is counter intuitive but it works like gang busters. Believe me. I've tried it and I've stick to this system for 4 years now.

Module 5 – How to Design Your Environment for Productivity

A Proven Step by Step Methodology to Getting the Things Out You Want from Life

by Leslie Abbott

Introduction

Well, my good friend, we are at the last module of our course. It's been a ride until here. The content itself was easy to go through but if you have actually done the exercises (you've done them, haven't you?), then this should have taken you at least 10 hours.

In this final module, we are going to talk about how you can use the environment to improve your productivity. As a gadget lover myself, I love to write about this. I love to write about how a single piece of software or the latest gadget can help you make more out of your life.

But if you're the kind of person who would rather keep it simple - then please, be my guest. A friend of mine, a brilliant copywriter decided to stop using his laptop and start using an old typewriter.

He loved writing copy on that thing. And I believe him. No Facebook, no Twitter, no Internet. You should try it too. A typewriter is 10% of the price of a computer.

So, let's get going and see how we can use technology and common sense to boost your working environment!

How the environment affects you

Some people can work in virtually any kind of environment. Most can't. Why? Because the wrong environment can send thousands of signals to the brain every hour that will affect your focus and clarity.

If you work in a place with a "bad vibe", whatever you may want to understand through this, no matter if it's a place with negative memories or just uncomfortable, your brain will always think about this, affecting your productivity dramatically.

For example, for a while, I've tried to work in some of the most inappropriate places possible. I was a wreck. Then one day I've decided to work a little in the park. It was like I came alive. The words just kept flowing. Even as I'm writing this right now, I'm listening to meditation music and today I've meditated twice.

And the words simply flow to the page. What does this mean to you?

It's simple. If you want to improve your results, improve your environment. Change the computer, change the desk, change the location. If you don't have the money, just go in the park with a pad of paper and write there. Do whatever it takes to be productive.

The brain can be a very strange system sometimes and you would be amazed how many things can change just because you've added a new photo on the wall or the lighting is different.

Designing your desk.

First of all, I don't suggest that you invest a lot of money in your desk. $100 is usually enough. Keep the expensive glass and aluminum desks for when you'll be rich.

But if you're going to get a quality desk, make sure it's big enough to fit your computer and at least a pad of paper. Then make sure it's tall enough to have a comfortable position at it. And finally, make sure that it looks nice so you'll enjoy working at it.

On your desk you should have only a few items. The more clutter you have the harder it will be for you to focus.

Ideally you should have a photo of your loved ones, a computer (laptop or desktop) and an inbox tray to deposit anything you need to process. This includes slips of paper, magazines and even books. Anything else is overkill and you can keep it into a drawer.

The rule of thumb here - the less items, the better.

Improving your office

Your office is the place where you'll spend most of your time. So, you may as well make it a second home. How do you improve your office?

I don't have a clear guideline but first of all, make sure you improve it based on the suggestions above. Second, make it personal. Add a painting. Add some flowers. Do whatever rocks your boat.

Third, eliminate anything that is not supposed to be there. As I've said, the fewer things in an office, the less thoughts will run rampant through your brains. Aim for minimalism if possible.

Fourth, forget about the normal mobile phone and buy a Bluetooth headset. This will save you a lot of time especially if using the phone is common business for you.

Fifth, add some good lighting. Lighting stimulates creativity and a well-lit office will make you feel better and less tired through the day.

These are just some suggestions. But in the end, the decision is yours. What's important is that you must do something to make it better in order to improve your productivity.

Ergonomics

When it comes to ergonomics, the rules are simple.

First, you should have at least 30 cm between your eyes and a display screen.

Second you should buy a keyboard that is easy to use and easy on the hands. This may cost a little more but it's worth it.

Third, every hour you should take a small break in order to relieve stress on your eyes.

Fourth, you need a good chair that will keep your spine straight.

Fifth, you should have some natural lighting from a window to keep your eyes healthy.

There are more rules than these but if you simply apply these ones, you'll feel a lot less stress by working in the office.

Using gadgets for productivity

My favorite part. Here I'm going to talk about the type of gadgets I've tried and my results with them.

First of all, the voice recorder. The voice recorder is a useful tool to have around, allowing you to record your thoughts, meetings and even phone conversations. But if you are not the kind of person that vocalizes his thoughts, then you'd better skip it. As far as the brand and price, I have a $100 voice recorder and it's perfect for my needs.

Second of all, tablet computer. While I enjoy using a tablet computer, they are not really fit for work. Instead, they act as a distraction, allowing you to check your Facebook feed once more. While sometimes they are very useful (as in reviewing a file), in the long term they'll waste more time than saving.

Third of all, smartphone. As a previous BlackBerry user, I'm tired of smartphones. Yes, having email on your phone is useful. Starting a task and stopping each time you get an email is not. Smartphones, especially those centered around email will train your mind to be distracted which is not a good thing. The best advice? Disable email or buy a cheap and durable phone.

There are a few more, which I'll only rate with one to five stars for their true utility:

Video projector ***

PDA **

Ebook reader ****

MP3 player *****

In the end, you don't need any of these things. But if you plan to buy some of them, be careful as the usual "business" tools may actually hurt your productivity.

Cut the internet connection

One of the biggest laughs I've got in my life was when a friend lost his wi-fi module for his laptop. I've thought that he's not going to get anything done until he bought another laptop.

Then what he did surprised me. He finished more work in one week than in the last two months combined. This made me think - how much time we spend on the Internet on junk websites?

The answer - way too much!

So, in my research to find a good solution for this, I've came across **Freedom** (https://freedom.to/splash.

This neat piece of software allows you to cut your Internet connection up to 480 minutes without being able to resume it (unless you restart your computer).

It costs $9 if you pay by the month or 3.33 if you pay for the whole year at once. And believe me, it's worth every penny.

But if you don't want to pay money for something like this, simply save everything you need from the web and then disable your router for a few hours. The world will not collapse in flames if you are not online for a few hours.

Exercise: Five ways to work without a computer

This is a simple and fun exercise. Think of five ways to get a project of yours done without using a computer (or tablet or mobile phone). Then pick up one method and get to work. You'll see that people can actually get things done without sitting in front of a keyboard all day.

Conclusion

It's been a long ride. But I'm glad that we've finished it. Now my friend, you have the tools and the valuable insight to become productive. Just apply what you've learned here and you'll get that project list done in no time.

Bonus 1 - "140 characters or less" tips on saving time

A Proven Step by Step Methodology to Getting the Things Out You Want from Life

by Leslie Abbott

Introduction

Dear friend,

I've thought about creating a quick list of tips that you can use to save time without going into great lengths about presenting them. Most of these can be called life hacks and you can use them from time to time to become more productive.

The Tips

- Use an Internet blocking utility as "Freedom (MacFreedom.com) to get some free time away from the Internet.

- If you can't stay without Internet, go into the Google Chrome shop and look for one of the many websites blocking software.

- Consider working in chunks of 30 minutes at a time to improve focus.

- Work in a well-lit area to improve creativity.

- Do not eat sugar in the morning or you'll lose your energy in about two hours.

- In the morning, drink half a liter of water to feel better.

- Shut down your phone each time you have a really important task to complete.

- Do one thing at a time and try to do it as good as you can - single tasking.

- Install software like Time Doctor (www.TimeDoctor.com) In order to see where you are really spending your time.

- Use Google Reader (reader.google.com) to gather all your websites in only one place.

- When buying general use items at the store, buy them in large quantities - you may never realize how much you are wasting each time you want to go out and buy another bottle of Cola.

- Try to not look into any kind of display, TV or otherwise, at least 30 minutes before sleeping.

- Get a Bluetooth headset in order to quickly answer calls on the move. Plus, it will improve your posture.

- Meditate at least 20 minutes a day in order to improve your focus.

- Take a break at least one day per week, even if you have a very busy agenda.

- At the start of each day, determine the top three things you want to accomplish today. Then start working on them.

- When in a meeting, set a clear duration for it. If it takes more, just leave. You have no energy for time wasters.

- Try to maximize dead time. For example, you can listen motivational tapes in your commute to work.

- Every time you feel overwhelmed, run. Running helps flush away every negative emotion.

- If you are a freelancer, consider using a project management platform to improve your productivity.

- Always keep a capture device with you, no matter if it's a voice recorder, a pad of paper or a smartphone. Write things down when you have to.

- At least once a day, spend some time alone. In this time, do not try to be productive. Do not try to create anything. Simply enjoy living.

- If you are in an environment where it's hard to work, better leave work until at the office. It's better to enjoy that time as your own than to do some work that needs to be redone anyway.

- If you have too many things to do in a certain day, pick up the most important 20% and do them. You can't do them all, so you may as well do what's truly important and let the others slip.

- If you discover that you need to do something, do not keep it in your mind. Email it to yourself, add it on a piece of paper or in your organizer. Your mind must be clear at all times.

- Productivity is not about getting as many things done as possible but rather producing good outcomes. Therefore, focus on each action with your full intensity to get it done in a great fashion instead of jumping from one to another.

- Classical music always helps improve focus, especially if you are studying or if you are working in a creative field.

- If you are really a productivity mess, consider closing down your social network accounts. This will give you about two hours per day of productive time.

- When in doubt of what to do next, start working on something. In the end, any work is better than no work.

- And most important - in order to be productive, you need a clear mind. If you can do this, then every task will become very, very easy.

Conclusion

I hope you've enjoyed this quick bonus. These are not fixed rules, but rather guidelines to help you live a stress free and more productive life. Now please take one of them and apply it.

Bonus 2 - Simple Project Planning

A Proven Step by Step Methodology to Getting the Things Out You Want from Life

by Leslie Abbott

Introduction

Dear friend,

Project planning is a complex science. It's so complex that unless you are a manager, you would find it dreadful to study it. However, there's an easy way. If you are a freelancer or if your project is not complex enough, you can plan a project in less than five minutes. How?

I'm going to show it to you here, in under a page.

Defining the outcome

Before you start a project, or anything at all for that matter, you need to know what you are after. You need to know how things will look at the end in order to be successful. How do you do that?

You simply write out the best-case scenario for that particular project. For example, if you want to go through a bathroom makeover, you will simply write how the bathroom will look like when this is done.

This will act as a quality standard on which to judge your work. Without a clear outcome, you are caught into the action steps and not in what you want to accomplish.

Brainstorming the tasks

This step is really simple. Write down every possible task you need to take in order to make this project a reality. By the end of it, you will have around 40 - 50 tasks. Do not group them yet, you are brainstorming.

Organizing the tasks

Now organize the tasks you've found above by days or by context. If you want to organize them by days, simply write when you are going to take care of them. If you want to organize them by context, write down in which context they will take place (example, at the computer, shopping, phone).

Allocating the tasks

Now you will take each task and allocate it to one or more people, if you are using a team. If not, you will simply use the plan from the step above.

Execution

This is the most painful step out of all. You will go through each task and complete it. Here is where most people fail. But if you complete the execution phase, the results will be good, even if your plan was average at least.

Conclusion

That's all. It's as simple as that. Now please take one of your projects and go through these steps to create a plan for achieving it.

Bonus 3 - Productivity Boosting Tools

A Proven Step by Step Methodology

to

Getting the Things Out You Want from Life

by Leslie Abbott

Introduction

This chapter came more as an afterthought. As you may know, you have already read my small review of tech gadgets in a previous module.

But I've thought that it would be a damn good idea to write a new bonus about how you can use each of these tools for the best results possible. So here, in this chapter, we are going to cover a best practice for each of the common productivity tools.

Voice recorder

A voice recorder in the right circumstances can be an amazing tool. Here is how you should use it. First of all, you should have it around at all times.

It's not really useful if you have an idea or a conversation to record and you've left it at home. Second, learn to use the pause function on the voice recorder instead of opening a new recording.

And third, do not worry about how you will sound on tape. Most of us sound awful. Focus on the content.

Now, that you've recorded what you want, you have two options. You can keep it in audio form or you can transcribe it. If you want to transcribe it, you can either hire someone to do it (it's on the pricey side, with around $3/minute) or do it yourself.

And if your voice is really, really clear, you can use a voice to text utility like Dragon Natural Speaking (http://www.nuance.com/dragon/index.htm) to have it automatically transcribed.

Journal

I highly suggest that you keep a journal. A journal can help you remember important thoughts and days and give you peace of mind.

I tend to use a paper journal as I like paper more. But if you are looking for a very good online solution, then go to www.penzu.com. It's the closest thing to paper I ever found.

And what's even better, it's free! There is also a paid version, with some neat options (like journaling by email), but if you want a free solution, don't look any more.

As far on how you should journal and how often, there are no clear rules. Journal once a day, when you feel like it. Talk about your day as you would talk to a friend, knowing that no one will ever read it.

Smartphone

If you want to purchase a smartphone, then here are a few great applications that you can use on it to become more productive.

The first one is Evernote. Evernote is an application that allows you to take notes in almost any form and size. It's something I use for years. If you'll use it on a phone, you can transform your photos in a note, you can record a voice note or you can quickly type a note with your phone's keyboard.

The second one is some kind of GTD application. I personally like Viira (https://www.kartamobile.com/viira.php) because it's very simple and it just works. Nowadays I'm not using my phone for GTD a lot, but when I've did, this app was a life saver.

The third one is a little different, as it's not a productivity app. This app is called Audible (www.audible.com). Audible is a marketplace for audiobooks. I've bought several books from that place, listened to them and became a lot more productive as a consequence. So if you are looking to improve yourself, the best place to start is Audible.com (these books are not cheap, but you can get a monthly subscription where you will get one book for around $8 and $14 after 3 months).

Tablet computer

While I strongly advise against buying a tablet computer, if you decide to do so, consider getting Skype for video calls, some kind of text editor (I'm just using Google Docs when I'm online) and a large supply of good books and motivational movies. That's as far as I can see a tablet computer being useful.

Virtual assistant

A VA is a person that you hire to take care of small tasks for you, like answering email, conducting research, etc.

They are cheap for the work they do but if you don't know how to use him or her efficiently, you'll lose a lot of money.

So, if I were to hire a VA once again, first of all, I would not look at the price but rather at the testimonials. A good track record tells a lot more than the price. And the second thing - at least the first few times, I would give precise instructions that even a monkey could follow. A VA cannot read your mind and if you just hope for the best, you'll pay for bad results.

Conclusion

These are good tools. But if you truly want to get things done, you can simply use a pad of paper and a pen. Remember that. Never use the lack of tools are an excuse for procrastination.